Count with the ancient Maya Calendar

*Maya calendar priests
called daykeepers have counted
the days since ancient times*

This full-figure glyph from Zoomorph B at the Maya site of Quirigua in Guatemala represents the interplay of two Maya time deities – god of the number 9 in red and the bak'tun bird (deity of a 144,000-day period) in green. Read as 9 bak'tuns, it represents a count of more than 3,500 years since Maya Creation Day, when the current Maya Era began. Head variant forms of the bak'tun and bearded number 9 glyphs can be seen on page 5 and inset on page 3.

Cover – sculptural representation from the basal register of Quirigua stela E of the same god of the number 9 illustrated in the full-figure glyph above.

© 2012 Ancientime. All rights reserved.
No part of this calendar may be reproduced in any form without permission of the author or publisher
ISBN: 978-0-9848865-2-4

The ancient Maya civilization

Head variant of the bak'tun *calendar glyph, representing a period of 144,000 days*

that flourished in pre-Columbian Mesoamerica between A.D. 250 – A.D. 900 is lauded today for its stunning intellectual achievements as much as for the remnants of exemplary art and architecture it left behind at archaeological sites all across the tropical lowlands and highland valleys of present-day Guatemala, Belize, and parts of Mexico, Honduras, and El Salvador. Perhaps, even more than for advanced astronomy, mathematics and hieroglyphic writing, the ancient Maya are best known for their fascination with time. As attested by dates recorded on stone monuments and in screen-fold bark paper books, the Maya calendar was an interlocking system of several component calendars which originated with earlier Mesoamerican cultures but were developed to their most elaborate and sophisticated forms by the Classic Period Maya.

Fervent astronomers and astrologers, the Maya formulated a holistic religious ideology that integrated astronomical observation with interpretation of the recurrent natural and agricultural cycles of their tropical world. They perceived time to be cyclic in nature and quantified it for daily life, primarily, with two intermeshed cyclical calendars – a 260-day count for ritual purposes called the *Tzolk'in* and a 365-day count for civil and agricultural purposes called the *Haab*. Other calendars counted lunar and planetary cycles.

Astronomical influence on the Maya calendar system is seen in the Lamat day sign, 8th of the 20 days in the Maya Tzolk'in calendar cycle. The central element within the cartouche symbolizes a star.

'El Caracol,' a rare cylindrical Maya structure with apparent astronomical alignments at the site of Chichén Itzá in Yucatan, Mexico, is believed to have been used as an observatory.

Left – A ruler's portrait on a stone monument at the Maya site of Arroyo de Piedra in present-day Guatemala.

0 mih   1 jun   2 ka'   3 ux   4 kan   5 ho'   6 wak

The k'in glyph depicts the Sun God and represents the solar day, as does the head variant sign for the number four

Maya mathematical proficiency brought Mesoamerican calendrics to their greatest level of precision and complexity, but Maya religious beliefs provided the force that, to their minds, kept the cycles of time in continual motion. The Maya counted the days and added them up into ever-larger intervals of time in belief that these chronological periods, and the numbers they counted them with, were living gods, whose interplay through time and space determined the fate or fortune of individual lives between birth and death.

Although Maya mathematicians usually recorded numbers with practical bar and dot symbols, the numbers 0–19 were sometimes depicted as the heads of custodial gods of time. In a few surviving examples, spectacular full figure forms were used which illustrate the Maya conception of how the gears of time were driven eternally forward. As if in a vast cosmic relay, deities associated with periods of time were depicted as burdens transferred from one custodial god to the next to keep the great cosmic mechanism in motion and time continually progressing from mythical past to unfathomable future.

Left – A portion of the beginning inscription from the Temple of the Cross at Palenque, Chiapas, Mexico. The left side paired glyph column is a mythical calendar date comprised of the 5 major time periods of the Maya Long Count calendar (12 bak'tuns, 19 k'atuns, 13 tuns, 4 winals, 0 k'ins) carved with head variant number coefficients. This is prelude to the significant event chronicled in the right side paired columns – the creation of our current world. The crucial Maya Calendar Round glyphs for that date – 4 Ajaw, 8 Kumk'u – are outlined in white.

An elaborate depiction of "16 days" from a Yaxchilan lintel. The monkey is a full-figure equivalent of the k'in glyph. He holds the head variant form of the number 6. The skull signifies 10.

Left & below: – Head variant forms of the Maya calendric number coefficients 0–13 representing custodial gods of time. After 12, the "teen" numbers used the same forms for 3–9 but modified by the addition of the skeletal lower jaw from the number 10. Equivalent bar/dot numbers included above.

7 huk   8 waxak   9 bolon   10 lajun   11 buluk   12 laj ka'   13 ox lajun

1 2 3 4 5 6 7 8 9 10

Vertical forms of Maya bar & dot numbers 1-19

Maya math

The Maya used a base 20 math system, perhaps derived from counting toes as well as fingers

Maya math used a vigesimal (base 20) positional notation system which allowed calculation of immense numbers by Maya scribes. Because they understood the important concept of zero, a quantity of any size could be expressed with only three basic symbols: a dot for one, a bar for five, and for zero, often a shell-like shape in manuscripts and a flower-like shape on carved stone monuments. Unlike our decimal system based on counting with ten fingers, the Maya system may have derived from counting with all twenty digits of a whole person, an idea reflected in the Ch'ol Mayan word, "winik," and the similar Yukatek Mayan word, "winal," which mean both "person" and "20" in their respective languages.

Maya dot numerals may have originally represented the finger tips used in counting, and the bars, a flattened hand. Mesoamerican merchants would have tallied valuable commodities such as cacao beans with a strictly vigesimal form of Maya math, but a modified system with eighteen (instead of twenty) 20-day months was used for calendar reckoning in order to more closely approximate the length of the solar year (18 x 20 = 360 days vs. 20 x 20 = 400 days). A special 5-day period was added at year's end to keep the 365-day *Haab* civil calendar reasonably aligned with the seasons.

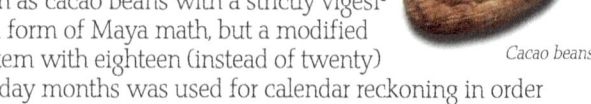

Cacao beans

With only one dot, the carved number at left is 6, not 8. In carved inscriptions, blank spaces were filled with decorative filler elements.

Numbers for calendric periods were usually carved with vertical bars and dots preceding time interval glyphs, while calculations on paper used horizontal bars and dots. Numbers 1–19 were written as concise bar-dot groupings, but beyond 19, number place values were stacked vertically upwards in increasing powers of 20 – *examples below.*

Merchant math – *Below are two examples of how large numbers would have been written for standard vigesimal math calculations, with successively higher place values stacked vertically (lines added for clarity). The shell-like symbol is a calligraphic form of zero.*

Calendrical math – *Entwined in the coils of a serpent, two large chronological counts from the Dresden Codex differ from the standard math examples below in that the third orders are multiples of 360, not 400. The black number (6 orders) accounts for 34,055 years; the red number equals 34,132 years. The rain deity Chaak emerges from the serpent.*

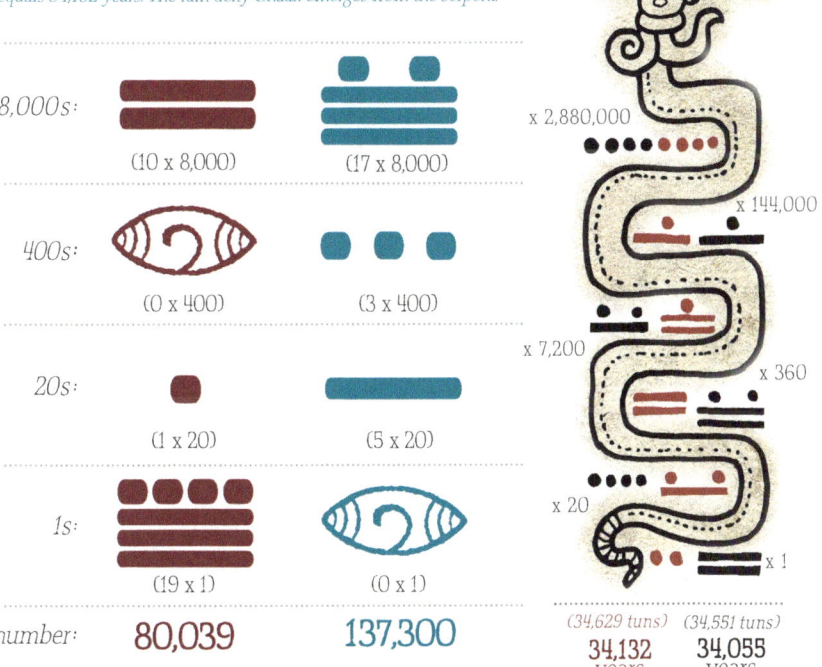

Right – At left of the top glyph block is the full-figure depiction of zero from Quirigua stela D. The diagnostic 'hand-on-jaw' and 'percentage sign' features are visible on arms and legs as it struggles with it's burden– the deity of the k'in (day) time period. The glyph block below represents the Tzolk'in position 7 Ajaw.

God of zero

Zero was conceived of by Mesoamerican mathematicians independently of its Old World origins and was personified as a Maya death god. Usually depicted with a hand over the jaw and often marked with a symbol like a percentage sign, zero represented more than nothingness for Maya calendars; it indicated the transition between the completion of one period of time and the start of another, as one custodial god transferred its temporal burden to the next.

One glyph variant for zero depicted a hand and snail-like shell to signify completion of a time interval. Another, the "chum" glyph, was derived from the stylized form of a seated lord and symbolized the installation, or "seating," of the next time period/god. It was used to designate the first day of a 20-day *Haab* month. This transitional transfer day is designated as zero and the remaining days as 1–19.

Calligraphic form

Flower form

Chum "seating" glyph

Completion form

"Seating" of Maya "month" of Mak (*0* Mak)

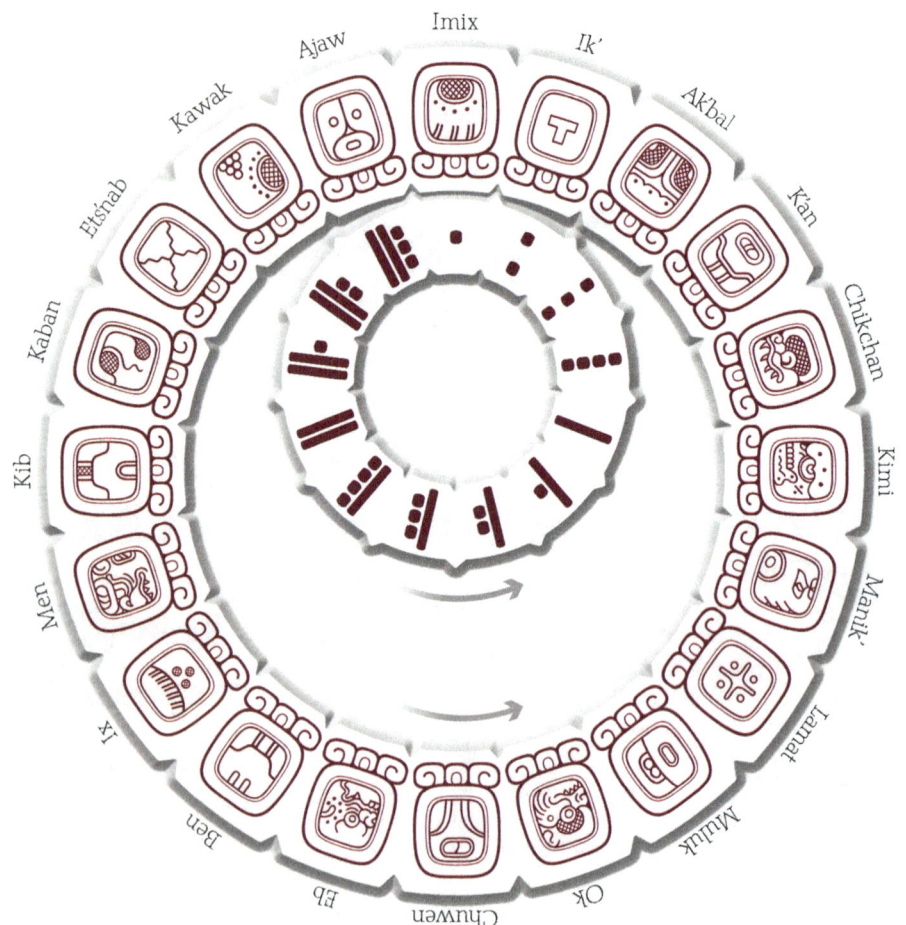

The 260-day Tzolk'in cycle
Graphic representation of the Tzolk'in as intermeshed cosmic gears.

Counting k'ins
The 260-day Tzolk'in ritual calendar cycle

6 Ajaw Tzolk'in date

K'in, the Mayan word for "day," also named the sun, and even time itself. There were 20 named days, each with its own distinct glyphic symbol, usually contained inside a day sign "cartouche" when inscribed on stone monuments. Day names and glyph elements varied over time period and cultural and linguistic region, but they are generally known today by the Mayan names transcribed by the Spanish in Colonial Period Yucatan, Mexico.

The sequence of 20 *k'ins* intermeshed with the numbers 1-13 to make up the 260-day (13 numbers x 20 days) Maya calendar cycle called the *Tzolk'in* ("Count of Days"). Also called the sacred or ritual almanac, this fundamental part of the Maya calendar system had truly ancient origins in early Mesoamerican cultures, yet is still used today by highland Maya daykeepers. As the two component cycles revolved together, the days and numbers were paired in sequence starting with 1 *Imix*, 2 *Ik*, 3 *Ak'bal*, and so on, cycling forward until 13 *Ben*. The number cycle then reverted to 1 so when the day cycle came around again to *Imix*, the count would be 8 *Imix*. This progression continued endlessly, arriving at the 1 *Imix* origin again once every 260 days

3 Eb Tzolk'in date

Highland Maya daykeepers have kept the Tzolk'in's order of days unbroken since ancient times and still use it in divination rituals at traditional ceremonial altar sites like the one called Paclóm outside Momostenango, Guatemala.

Maya day glyphs

The true ancient origins of Maya calendar glyphs are lost to time and the tragedies of conquest, but, over the last century, Mayanists have attempted to refit as much as possible of this complex puzzle. The information on potential meanings or origins of day signs offered on these pages was derived, in part, from J. Eric Thompson's Maya Hieroglyphic Writing. *Still regarded as a master ethnographer, some of his hieroglyphic work has been questioned since the time of his writing in 1950 prior to many advances in epigraphic studies. His calendrical glyph conjectures are still valuable, but the subject continues to be re-evaluated by modern Mayanists. Day signs are presented in sequence by column below.*

Ajaw day sign glyph in its most elaborate, full figure form.

Imix is a stylized image of a water lily and represents an aquatic earth monster /deity which floats like a crocodile under the lily covered surface of a primordial body of water.

Ik' represents wind of all forms, including breath and, therefore, life.

Ak'bal portrays a stylized segment of a snake with its belly scales and part of its upper body pattern. It represents the darkness of the Maya Underworld.

K'an symbolizes a ripe kernel of maize, the main source of sustenance for the Maya. The Mayan word *k'an* means yellow.

Chikchan, in personified form represents the head of a celestial serpent, a deity of rain & storms.

Kimi, in symbolic form, resembles a percentage sign. Its personified form is the skull of the death god, often with this "percentage sign" mark on it.

Manik' is commonly represented as a hand gesture with thumb & forefinger tips touching. This was, perhaps, a hunter's silent hand sign for "deer".

Lamat is a star sign which can also represent the planet Venus.

 **Muluk** is associated with the precious commodities of jade and water.

 Ok, in personified form, is the head of a dog deity who guided the sun through the Underworld every night. It often has a ragged, torn ear.

 **Chuwen**, in addition to this symbolic form, also has a personified form as a howler monkey, probably the image of *Hun Chuwen*, one of the monkey twin patron gods of scribes, artists, and craftsmen.

 **Eb**, in personified form with its fleshless jawbone, resembles the death god image of the *Kimi* day sign, though less skull-like. It represents a malignant rain deity which sends the mist and mildew that destroy crops.

 **Ben** resembles the *K'an* day sign's maize kernel symbol. Perhaps, it represents growing maize as opposed to *K'an*'s ripe maize.

 **Ix** resembles Imix but its spots indicate an association with jaguars instead of water lilies. *Hix* is a Mayan word for jaguar.

 Men is a deity, sometimes with the beak-like snout of a raptorial bird. The equivalent Aztec day sign is an eagle.

 **K'ib** resembles an inverted *K'an* day sign. It may represent a conch shell, as does the main sign of the glyph for the cardinal direction, "south".

 **Kaban** represents the earth. Its curly shapes, reminiscent of sprouting seeds, are also found on the head variant form of the number 11 glyph. Its Aztec equivalent day sign represents movement, such as from earthquakes.

 Ets'nab is a stylized image of a pressure flaked flint or obsidian knife or spear head. It, perhaps, is a deity associated with human sacrifice.

 **Kawak** has a "grape cluster" element that may depict rain clouds but the overall symbol represents "stone" in Maya art.

 **Ajaw**, in its personified form, depicts a young Maya lord. This more common form is the stylized face of the Sun God. The Mayan word, *Ajaw*, means "Lord."

The 365-day Haab cycle
Represented here as an ever-revolving cosmic cogged wheel, it is more difficult to visualize than the Tzolk'in because that sequence of 20 numbered days cycled within each Haab month. It would require a 365-position wheel to fully illustrate its complete set of day & number pairings. (See Calendar Round illustration on following pages)

Counting winals
The 365-day Haab cycle

The Maya used a 365-day calendar cycle called the *Haab* to keep track of civil matters and seasonal agricultural cycles. On this order of calendric math, the base 20 system was modified to approximate the length of the solar year by creating eighteen 20-day months instead of twenty. To arrive at 365 days, a special 5-day period called *Wayeb* was added at the end of the year. It was considered an unlucky period when many normal activities were suspended.

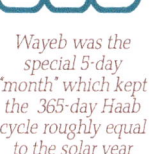

Wayeb was the special 5-day 'month' which kept the 365-day Haab cycle roughly equal to the solar year

"*Winal*" was the Mayan word for the 20-day month. As with *Tzolk'in* day names, the *Haab* month names varied by cultural region and *winal* signs were depicted with both abstract and personified symbols, some with origins so distant their meanings are difficult to discern with certainty. The days of each *winal* within the *Haab* were assigned one of a cycling sequence of 20 numbers, but their counting was complicated by the deified aspect of Maya time. The transition day between consecutive months was ruled by the god of zero, so the *k'ins* in months of twenty days were numbered 0–19 instead of 1–20 and the 5 *k'ins* in *Wayeb*, 0–4. Thus, 0 *Pop*, the first day of the Maya *Haab* year, was when *Pop's* influence was first felt but the second day, 1 *Pop*, was when it ruled in full force. The "*chum*" glyph, used to proclaim the installation, or "seating," of a new ruler, was also used as a zero coefficient to designate the seating of a new *winal*.

13 Muwan Haab date

"seating" of Mak (0 Mak)

Rare dog's head form of the K'ank'in winal glyph with coefficient number 6

Maya month glyphs

The toad/frog's head symbol pictured at right is a common form of the Maya Long Count calendar glyph representing the 20-day winal "month" period of the 365-day Haab calendar cycle. Presented in sequence by column below are versions of the individual winal glyphs with information on their possible origins or meanings.

 **Pop**
Pop was the first month of the Maya *Haab* year. Pop is a Mayan word for "mat" and the woven mat design was a symbol of authority, such as for the seating place (throne) of a ruler. The infixed "k'an cross" symbol means "precious" or "yellow."

 **Wo** –*Black sky*–
The crossed bands main sign is a celestial symbol. The "ek" superfix above it represents the color black.

 **Sip** –*Red sky*–
The crossed bands main sign is a celestial symbol. The "chak" superfix above it represents the color red.

 **Sots'**
The head variant form of Sots' is a leaf-nosed bat which has an ear-like skin flap above the nose to aid echolocation.

 **Sek**
Sek's superfix, main sign and subfix components phonetically spell "ka-se-wa," the Ch'ol and, perhaps, its Classic period Mayan name.

 **Xul**, Xul's head variant form is a rodent-like mammal. The tail-like subfix element is the final syllable "ni" of the Ch'ol Mayan name for the month, "chi-chin-ni," as it is written phonetically.

 **Yaxk'in**
–*New or first sun*–
The main sign is the sun glyph, k'in. The "yax" superfix sign represents a range of colors between blue and green but can also mean "new." The tail-like subfix element is part of the final syllable of "yax-k'in-ni" as it is written phonetically.

 **Mol**
Mol spells itself phonetically ("mo-lo") in both Yukatek and Ch'ol Mayan. The dotted outer ring, "mo," surrounds the central element, "lo," which is also the day sign, Muluk.

Ch'en
Ch'en is the first of four months with a Kawak (stone) main sign. Its *"ek"* superfix signifies black, the directional color for West. An alternate Mayan name is *"Ek Sihom."*

Yax
Yax is the second of four months with a Kawak (stone) main sign. The yax superfix can signify "new" or a blue/green range of colors. An alternate Mayan name is *"Yax Sihom."*

Sak
Sak is the third of four months with a Kawak (stone) main sign. Its *"sak"* superfix signifies white, the directional color for North. An alternate Mayan name is *"Sak Sihom."*

Keh
Keh is the fourth of four months with a Kawak (stone) main sign. Its *"chak"* superfix signifies red, the directional color for East. An alternate Mayan name is *"Chak Sihom."*

Mak
Mak's personified form has a superfix of the syllable "ma" and the head of the Xoc fish as a main sign which can be read as "ka." Together, the name of the month is spelled phonetically (*"ma-ka"*).

Kank'in
Although K'ank'in's rare head variant form is a dog, this common tree-like symbolic form may represent a gourd. The circle's crosshatching represents the color black.

Muwan
Image of the mythical Moan bird. Although often depicted as owl-like, it is, perhaps, based on a sparrow hawk and sometimes holds the feet and feathers of its prey in its beak.

Pax
The central part of the Pax glyph is a *"tun"*, the symbolic-form glyph for the Maya Long Count 360-day time period. The tun symbol represents a Maya log drum and the scroll-like shape emanating from it may represent the drum's sound.

Kayab
K'ayab's parrot-like beaked head may actually be a turtle. The "k'an cross" sign infixed in the eye means "yellow" or "precious." The glyph components phonetically spell *"k'an-a-si,"* the Ch'ol Mayan name for the month.

Kumk'u
Kumk'u's main sign is the K'an day glyph which, perhaps, represents a maize kernel. The superfix above it may represent a feather.

Wayeb
Wayeb was the 5-day unlucky period at the end of the Maya *Haab* year. Like the Pax glyph, the main sign is a *"tun,"* the symbolic form for the 360-day period of the Long Count Calendar. The superfix sign above it represents the pincers of a *"chapat"*, a centipede.

Counting eternity
The 18,980-day Calendar Round cycle

The 260-day *Tzolk'in* cycle intermeshed with the 365-day *Haab* cycle into an 18,980-day (52-year) cycle now known as the Calendar Round. This was the interval required for any particular numbered day and month pairing, such as 2 *Ik' 0 Pop*, to reoccur and was sufficient to account, with limited repetition of dates, for the major affairs of an average individual's lifetime. Although, in the Maya system, the Calendar Round intermeshed with ever-greater cycles of time, day counting was restricted to the length of the Calendar Round cycle in some Mesoamerican cultures such as the Aztecs, who suffered such anxiety that time would stop at the cycle's end that they performed a special New Fire Ceremony to insure against the prospect.

6 Ajaw 13 Muwan Calendar Round date

As illustrated at right, a common modern metaphor for the mechanics of the Calendar Round is that of a series of cosmic cogged wheels which inexorably click off the eternal march of time, one *k'in* at a time. In turn, the Calendar Round can be envisioned to drive the immense cycles of the Maya Long Count, representing extraordinary, even incomprehensible, intervals of time.

4 Ajaw 8 Kumk'u
Calendar Round for the mythic Maya Creation Day

The Aztec calendar system derived from the same MesoAmerican origins as the Maya and, likewise, had a 52-year cycle comprised of day and month cycles analogous to those of the Maya system. This stone Xiuhmolpilli monument depicts a bundle of 52 reeds representing the 52-year Aztec Calendar Round. 52 reed bundles were burned in the New Fire Ceremony at the close of each Calendar Round in the hope of keeping the cycle in motion and the world in order. The affixed Aztec day sign 2 Acatl (2 reed) names the final year of the cycle and equates with the Maya day sign Ben.

At right – a graphic representation of the 4 Ajaw 3 Kank'in Calendar Round date for the completion of a 13-bak'tun / 5,125-year Maya time period on December 21, 2012 A.D. Gregorian. The Haab wheel shown in portion at right would have 365 positions for its cycle of numbered days. To fully illustrate the complete 13-bak'tun cycle would require envisioning ever-larger, immense enmeshed wheels for the k'atun and bak'tun time cycles of the Maya Long Count.

260-day Tzolk'in cycle with 13-number and 20-day component cycles

365-day Haab cycle with 18 winals of 20 numbered days and the 5-day *Wayeb* period

Counting creations
The infinite Maya Long Count

In order to link historical events into grander temporal cycles, the Maya tracked linear time with what Mayanists now call the Long Count, most frequently found inscribed on stelae, carved stone monuments erected to mark time and commemorate the achievements and exploits of rulers.

Although it meshed with the Calendar Round and other more esoteric cycles, the Long Count calendar was distinct as a count of days since a specific starting point – the mythic Maya Creation Day. Mayanists have been able to correlate the Maya Long Count with the calendar we now use and calculate back to determine that August 11, 3114 B.C. Gregorian. was the day the Maya believed a previous Era concluded and our current world was created by powerful gods.

Following from that "zero" date, most historical dates in Maya inscriptions fall within the nearly-400-year period between AD 435 and AD 825 comprising the 9th *bak'tun* of the Maya Long Count Calendar. Most inscriptions begin with such dates in a distinctive format Mayanists refer to as the "initial series" (*illustrated on following pages*). Maya scribes moved forward and backward in time in inscriptions by means of "distance numbers," which were added or subtracted from the initial series date to refer to earlier historic, future prophetic, or mythical events. Actions of rulers were often depicted as reenactments of primordial gods. Some mythical dates reach back far, far before modern science's roughly fourteen billion-year estimate of the age of the universe.

Long Count time periods

Long Count dates usually included the five orders of time illustrated below in their head variant glyph forms, progressing from the *k'in* (1 day) at the bottom up to the *bak'tun* (144,000 *k'ins*). Listed above are the next four orders of Long Count time beyond the *bak'tun*, as they are ascribed by Mayanists. The highest of these, the *alawtun*, would account for more than 63,000,000 years! Occasionally, the Maya referenced even far greater increments of time.

Maya stelae were erected by rulers to commemorate their exploits and usually featured their portraits front and back. Inscriptions down the sides commenced with a Long Count date in order to establish their place in historical and mythical time. Shown at left is Copán Stela A, which portrays the ruler Waxaklajun Ub'ah K'awil, sometimes referred to as "Eighteen Rabbit."

The Long Count on Stela 10 at Tikal in Guatemala includes the rare 3 higher orders of time above the usual 5 illustrated at right. Descending from the top is shown a count of 1 k'inchiltun, 11 kalabtuns, 19 piktuns. Their values in k'ins / days are listed above at right. Their sum is more than 5 million years.

Alawtun
20 *k'inchiltuns*
23,040,000,000 *k'ins* / *days*

K'inchiltun
20 *kalabtuns*
1,152,000,000 *k'ins* / *days*

Kalabtun
20 *piktuns*
57,600,000 *k'ins* / *days*

Piktun
20 *bak'tuns*
2,880,000 *k'ins* / *days*

Bak'tun
20 *k'atuns*
144,000 *k'ins* / *days*

sometimes represented as a mythical bird with a hand covering or replacing the lower jaw

K'atun
20 *tuns*
7,200 *k'ins* / *days*

sometimes represented as a mythical bird but also as a wooden drum form

Tun
18 *winals*
360 *k'ins* / *days*

personified here as a mythical bird with a skeletal human mandible and a jaguar's ear and eye

Winal
20 *k'ins* / *days*

often represented in head variant form as a frog or toad but also as an abstract symbol

K'in
1 *k'in* / day

sometimes depicted as a flower form but often personified as the Sun God

Maya Creation Day inscription

Referred to by archaeologists as Stela C, a still-standing 12-foot tall sandstone monument was erected in AD 775 at the Guatemalan Maya site of Quirigua by its eighth-century king, *K'ak' Tiliw Chan Yo'pat*. Its east side hieroglyphic inscription starts with the significant Long Count date for the start, on August 11, 3114 BC Gregorian, of the current Maya Era and the creation of the world we still live in. Although a propaganda exercise to place his reign in context of cosmic time cycles, it resulted in preserving the most complete Classic Period account of Maya Creation mythology, which describes how powerful gods worked together to set up the cosmic order and the current, perhaps nearly complete, 5,125-year Maya Creation cycle. This, and other shorter parallel inscriptions, combined with mythological imagery from pre-Columbian Maya pottery and references in the few surviving Maya manuscripts, provide a background for understanding the current phenomenon of intense interest in the Maya calendar and the year 2012.

A recurring theme, especially evident on Stela C, employs a compelling metaphor comparing the grand ordering of the cosmos to the construction of a humble Maya house, commencing with the placement of a simple three-stone hearth at its center.

Quirigua Stela C south face.

As usual with Maya stelae, Stela C portrays the ruler who erected it in ceremonial costume to promote his status as a divine king. On the south face, shown here, K'ak' Tiliw is depicted as an actor in the mythological drama of the east side inscription (shown at far right and enlarged on page 22). Across his chest, he holds an image of the Jaguar-throne stone described in the Creation text. His costumery is rich in symbolism of warfare and power. The last glyph block at far right under his feet names the monument as 'The 6-Ajaw Stone', a reference to the Tzolk'in date of its erection.

Stela C names the cosmic counterparts as jaguar-, serpent-, and water-throne stones, platforms from which several deities collaborated on their epic task at a location named as "First three-stone place." Ethnographic research in modern-day highland Guatemala suggests that the ancient Maya may have seen a triad of stars in the Orion constellation as the locus of this mythological event.

Simulation of the 3-stone hearth found in traditional Maya houses for millennia – basis for the Creation myth metaphor on Quirigua Stela C.

It is thought that the Maya saw the three stars we see as Orion's belt as the "turtle constellation." An image of a turtle bearing three stones, illustrated in celestial context in the Madrid Codex, suggests a triad of stars within Orion as the mythic place where the Maya Creation event occurred.

Glyph block near the east side base of Stela C, which names the place of Creation as "First three-stone place." A stack of three stones is seen in its lower right corner.

Quirigua Stela C east side text

Maya Creation Day inscription

As described and illustrated on the next page, the first third of the inscription is taken up by the 13.0.0.0 Long Count date, which is then followed by the Calendar Round's Tzolk'in and Haab calendar glyphs.

4 Ajaw 8 Kumk'u
Calendar Round for the mythical
Maya Creation Day

Two deities named as participants in the Stela C creation account were Jaguar Paddler and Stingray Paddler. The latter sports a stingray spine through his nasal septum.

Following the calendar information, the remainder of the inscription lists four gods, who, working under the supervision of another, set about to reorder the cosmos from a celestial location called 'First three-stone place.' As usual for Maya monument texts, the story is told in a terse, formal style, with limited details given. However, close variations of this account, describing the same basic event, appear on enough Maya monuments and painted ceramics to indicate that a variable, but generally culture-wide mythology is being presented.

Long Count & Calendar Round dates from Quirigua Stela C east side hieroglyphic text.

Long Count dates began with an introducing glyph which incorporated an image of the patron deity for the Calendar Round month. The paired glyph blocks that follow it are read left to right, then down, in zig-zag fashion.

13 bak'tuns
(13 x 144,000 days = 1,872,000 days)

0 k'atuns
(0 x 7,200 days = 0 days)

0 tuns
(0 x 360 days = 0 days)

0 winals
(0 x 20 days = 0 days)

0 k'ins
(0 x 1 day = 0 days)

4 Ajaw
(Tzolk'in date)

8 Kumk'u
(Haab date)

This Long Count date covering the standard 5 orders of time is written by Mayanists as 13.0.0.0.0.

Jaguar & Stingray Paddler gods

The inscription continues in another 19 glyph blocks after the Long Count (red) and Calendar Round (green) date glyphs with an account of how certain gods worked together to set up the fourth and current world order and a now nearly complete, 5,125-year Maya time period.

Counting deep time

The current misconception that the Maya calendar will end and the ancient Maya predicted an end to time itself, are not based on the archaeological record and more than a century's worth of scholarship, so serious Maya scholars dismiss such ideas entirely. A matter still in debate, however, is the structure of the Long Count's component cycles, such as whether *bak'tuns* recycle in series of 13 or 20. If 13, December 21, 2012 will initiate the restart to *bak'tun* 1 in a new series of 13. If 20, we will instead move into the 14th *bak'tun* with 7 more *bak'tuns* (2,760 years) left to reach the first *piktun* (20 *bak'tuns*) forward from that date. Other more complicated structures have been proposed, but whatever the details of the mechanism, overall evidence suggests the Maya expected a perpetually enduring future, even though the culture and political structure of the Classic Period Maya did not last to enter it.

One can only speculate on what calendrical knowledge or beliefs were lost when Maya books were burned by Spanish priests, but Maya monumental inscriptions were written to validate rulers in respect to their predecessors, or, better still, to the ancient gods in primordial time, so they mostly projected backwards. A few surviving examples reveal the great immensity of deep time considered by ancient Maya scribes and present a puzzle for modern Mayanists to ponder. Foremost of these is a badly eroded extended Long Count on Stela 1 at the site of Cobá in present-day Quintana Roo, Mexico.

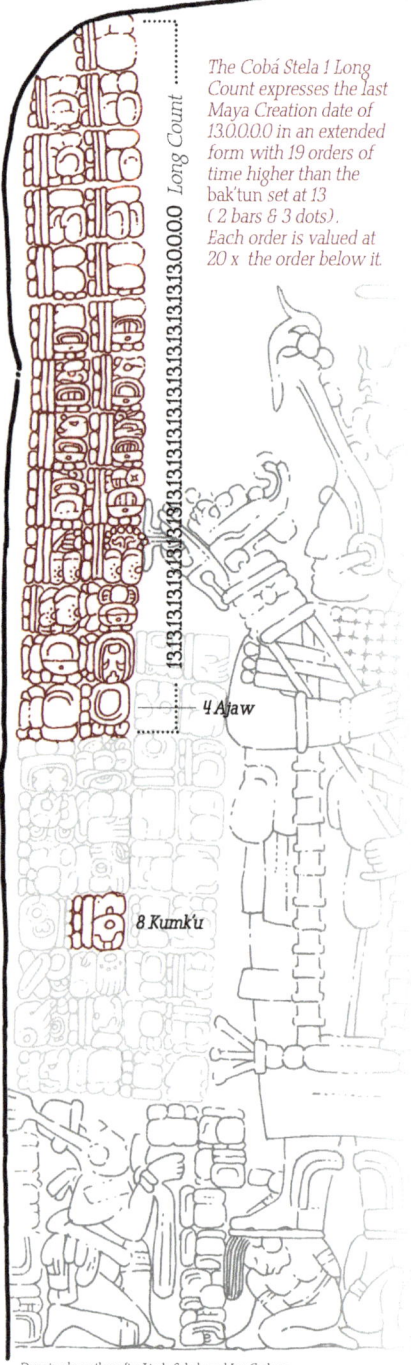

The Cobá Stela 1 Long Count expresses the last Maya Creation date of 13.0.0.0.0 in an extended form with 19 orders of time higher than the bak'tun set at 13 (2 bars & 3 dots). Each order is valued at 20 x the order below it.

Drawing by author after Linda Schele and Ian Graham

Expanding from the 5 orders of time usually found in Long Count inscriptions, the Cobá stela 1 Long Count is written with 19 higher orders, each one 20x its predecessor. It references the date of the last Creation when 13 previous *bak'tuns* had concluded. Mayanists write the usual occurrences of this date as 13.0.0.0.0 but this Cobá instance is written as 13.13.13.13.13.13.13.13.13.13.13.13.13.13.13. 13.13.13.13.0.0.0.0. This represents a period of time so incomprehensibly vast that the modern scientific estimate of the age of the universe as roughly 14 billion years amounts to only a very tiny fraction of one percent of it! 13 was a numerologically significant number to the Maya, so this astounding, preposterously expanded Long Count was likely intended for symbolic emphasis of the significance of the ruler's actions tied to it.

Several magnificently carved stelae at the site of Quirigua in present-day Guatemala have extensive inscriptions referencing deep mythological time. The example at left, the well-preserved East side inscription of Stela F, shifts backwards and forwards through millions of years to provide mythological context and validation to the momentous action of Quirigua's ruler, *K'ak' Tiliw*, in capturing and decapitating the ruler of the larger, more powerful city of Copán on May 3, AD 738.

Quirigua Stela F East side hieroglyphic text. Glyph blocks with higher-order time periods are keyed to their descriptions below.

A – 0 alawtuns (1 alawtun = over 63 million years)
B – 19 x 20^7 tuns completed (roughly 24 trillion years) (20^7 tuns = 20 alawtuns)
C – 0 pictuns (1 pictun = about 7,885 years)
D – 13 kalabtuns (over 2 million years)
E – decapitation (the x-shaped element in the top right corner of this glyph block represents a stone axe, instrument for decapitation)

Completion of the 13th bak'tun on December 21, 2012

Glyphs for "13 bak'tuns completed" inscribed on Palenque's Temple of the Cross tablet, from a text passage recounting the creation of the current Maya Era, on August 11, 3114 BCE. The same glyphs could apply to the subsequent completion of 13 more bak'tuns beyond that base date on December 21, 2012.

The much anticipated completion of the Maya calendar's thirteenth bak'tun cycle will occur on December 21, 2012. If you are reading this after that date, it should be abundantly clear that the rumors of ancient prophecies and all manner of looming cosmic catastrophes have gone the way of Y2K and many other apocalyptic fantasies. Those that thrive on such creative speculations will now have to find a new date to focus on and contrive new theories to fear and profit from.

It's important to note that serious pre-Columbian scholars have assuredly proclaimed all along there was no archaeological basis for any of the phenomenal 2012 hysteria. In fact, the rampant apocalyptic aspect of it reflects Christian, rather than Mesoamerican concepts. Although surviving Maya mythology recounts the destruction of 3 previous world ages, the context was not of an end to time, but rather of the gods correcting previous creations until they were successful with creating humans to worship them. A great deal of evidence suggests the Maya's core belief of the nature of time was that it was endlessly cyclical.

Although the basic mechanics of Maya calendrics have been well understood for the last century and advances in Maya epigraphy (the study of hieroglyphs) in recent decades have lifted many mysteries concerning ancient Maya writings, no known inscription or Pre-Columbian manuscript indicates the Maya predicted a "doomsday" or, actually, much of anything to occur in 2012. In fact, although many ancient references to the beginning of the current Maya Era exist, only two are known to include its possible closing date. One of those was

A photo-reconfiguration of stucco glyphs from Palenque simulates what the calendar round of 4 ajaw 3 k'ankin will be on 12/21/12.

One of only two known occurrences of the 12/21/2012 date in Maya inscriptions is on a fragmented panel from the now-destroyed site of Tortuguero in Mexico. Illustrated at left, the final 8 glyph blocks announce the completion of 13 bak'tuns on the Calendar Round date 4 Ajaw 3 Kank'in but damage to the last few glyph blocks obscures the meaning of events foretold for the day. The god, Bolon Yokte', is mentioned with the dog-like glyph that phonetically spells the 'ok' part of his name.

Author drawing after Sven Grönemeyer and Mark Van Stone, and photos by Donald Hales and Elisabeth Wagner

only just discovered in Guatemala in the summer of 2012 but the date within a larger glyphic text only provides a bare chronological point of reference with no prophecy or drama attached to it.

The only other known Classic Period inscription that includes the 2012 date is found on three fragments of the closing passage of a T-shaped monument from the 7th-century site of Tortuguero in Tabasco, Mexico. Unfortunately, although the incomplete, damaged date glyphs can still be discerned, missing portions of the following final four glyph blocks preclude definitive translation of what is to occur on that date involving an obscure god, believed to be an agent of transition, including events occurring at calendar period-endings. However, an in-depth evaluation of the inscription by master epigraphers* suggested that, on December 21, 2012, this god, *Bolon Yokte'*, would be adorned in his best ceremonial attire on the occasion of a ritual commemoration of an ancient building dedication. Nothing apocalyptic seems to be on the agenda for the day.

Also, importantly, some Mayanists believe the previous 13-*bak'tun* cycle was unique and our current Era will close only at the completion of 20 *bak'tuns* (1 *piktun*), 2,760 years from 12/21/2012. A 20-*bak'tun* cycle would be more compatible with the Long Count's primarily vigesimal structure, and would give doomsayers another 7 *bak'tuns*/2,760 years to worry about.

At Palenque, an extensive inscription on the funerary temple of the most famous of Maya kings, K'inich Janaab Pakal, uses the glyph for 1 piktun (equal to 7,885 years) to cast a date forward far past 2012 to AD 4,772.

Maya rulers manipulated time in inscriptions to legitimize political power in reference to history and mythology. They usually reached into the deep past, but a few inscribed dates far beyond 2012 clearly suggest the Maya did not believe the future would end then. Foremost of these, a lengthy text carved on Palenque's Temple of Inscriptions confidently states that the accession of the ruler, *K'inich Janaab Pakal*, will be commemorated in AD 4,772 – 2,760 years beyond 2012! This would imply that we will move safely forward into bak'tun 14.

*An extensive analysis of Tortuguero Monument 6 by Sven Grönemeyer and Barbara MacLeod can be found at http://www.wayeb.org/notes/wayeb_notes0034.pdf in the archives of the European Association of Mayanists website at: http//www.wayeb.org/

Lords of Time

S telae were the ultimate expression of concepts of time pervasive in Classic period Maya culture. With Long Count dates inscribed as much as a millennium and a half ago, the stelae that survive today have truly fulfilled their intended purpose as markers of time. For modern archaeologists, they have preserved a sophisticated ancient writing system and provided a historical framework for understanding the royal culture and mythology of a remarkable civilization.

Maya kings erected stelae and other monuments on period-ending dates dictated by the mathematics of the calendar. The Mayan word *tuun* (stone) is included in the term *lakam tuun* (large stone)

A bench support from Copán portrays a Maya lord holding a feather-decorated, obsidian-bladed bloodletter for use in blood sacrifice / vision quest rituals.

The ajaw glyph, symbol both for a Maya lord and the day that completes the Tzolk'in's 20-day cycle. The conflation suggests a belief in a Maya ruler's power in both earthly and celestial realms.

for "stela" and indicates a conceptual association with the *tun* (360-day "year") and *katun* (20 *tuns*) time periods incessantly commemorated by the setting of stelae/stones. *Katuns*, especially, were observed, as well as three-quarter *katun*, half *katun* (*hotun*) and quarter *katun* periods. All Long Count period-endings have coefficients of zero for the *winal* and *k'in* positions.

The primary sculptural element of a stela was usually a formal portrait depicting the ruler who commissioned it in ritual performance of his royal duty as spiritual conduit to the Otherworld of gods and ancestors. His ceremonial costumery, including an elaborate headdress or deity mask, incorporated symbols of earthly and celestial power. Often, the ruler was portrayed as if in a trance state with deities or ancestors emerging from vision serpents conjured from the smoke of his royal offerings.

All this rich imagery was intended to proclaim to his subjects and the gods how he fulfilled his obligations to maintain the continuum of order of sacred space and time. Like the gods of the calendar glyphs, he was a Lord of Time.

An alternate ajaw glyph takes the form of a vulture's head. This beautifully carved example is from a Tikal temple lintel with a very rare surviving inscription in wood.

Copán stela P portrays the ruler K'ak' Chan Yopaat, who reigned for 50 years until his death in AD 628. Many Maya stelae depict rulers in profile, but those at the nearby and interrelated sites of Copán and Quiriguá favored direct frontal views carved in more ornate, deeply cut styles than those found at other Maya sites. Deity mask headdresses and other ceremonial costume elements were densely packed with political and mythological symbols. A prominent recurring object is what Mayanists refer to as a "double-headed serpent bar," a scepter-like object clutched across the chest by a distinctive claw-like gesture of the hands, which never actually grasp the object.

Deity mask headdress

A cosmological explanation for serpent bars is as representations of the ecliptic and Maya rulers on stelae as symbols of the Milky Way.

Jaguar Paddler god

Double-headed serpent bar.
Usually rigid, scepter-like in form, sometimes they are flexible, and snake-like, as in this example which loops down the chest.

As conduits from the Otherworld, gods and ancestors invoked during blood sacrifice rituals performed by rulers are shown materializing from both ends. In this case, the emerging gods are the same paddler gods who were key players in the Creation mythology recounted on Quiriguá stela C.

Stingray Paddler god

Myth and history in stone

The art for each month in this calendar features photography of some of the most magnificent examples of monumental Maya sculpture. Particularly represented are two eighth-century Maya kings of the nearby and interrelated sites of Copán and Quirigua in present-day Honduras and Guatemala. Although stela inscriptions seek validation by reference to mythological events in primordial time, they also record actual history. A notable example is the treacherous story boasted on several massive stelae by Quirigua's ruler *K'ak' Tiliw* of the capture and beheading of his former overlord, *Waxaklahun Ubah K'awil*, king of the larger ancient city of Copán, on May 3, 738. Inscriptions at Copán confirm the loss of this important ruler.

"Decapitation" glyph from Quirigua stela F. The X-shaped object at top represents a stone axe.

Copán stela A, one of several monumental portraits of Waxaklahun Ubah K'awil. His name glyph is shown below, which means something like "eighteen names or manifestations of the god K'awil".

Name glyph of K'ak' Tiliw Chan Yopat, which translates approximately as "Fire-burning celestial lightning god. Quirigua stela D presents one of his several portraits there.

Gregorian / Maya calendar correlation

Although the Long Count was based on a mid-August start date, the *Haab* calendar's original correlation to solar seasons can't be known for sure. The Maya system did not account for leap years, so the first day of the *Haab* cycle, 0 Pop, has continually drifted by one day every four years. During the Maya Classic Period, the *Haab* year began close to the vernal equinox but has drifted more than an entire solar year since then and falls on 2 *Ik'* 0 *Pop*, April 2 Gregorian in 2013.

This calendar uses the commonly accepted Goodman, Martinez, Thompson (GMT) Gregorian/Maya correlation. By use of historical, astronomical, and other evidence, this formula determined that the completion of the previous Maya Age occurred on August 11, 3114 BCE Gregorian or Julian day number (JDN) 584283. For those who prefer the modified GMT (+2 days) correlation based on JDN 584285, all Maya dates in this calendar would occur two Gregorian days later than printed here. For example, 0 *Pop*, the first day of the *Haab* year, falls on Gregorian April 2, 2013 according to the GMT correlation but would fall on Gregorian April 4, 2013 with the GMT+2 correlation. Likewise, the completion of the 13th *bak'tun* occurs on December 23 with GMT+2, instead of December 21, 2012 with the GMT correlation.

2 Ik' 0 Pop
First day of the Haab year falls on April 2 Gregorian in 2013 with the GMT correlation

Spelling note for Mayan words

"Mayan" is sometimes used in this calendar in a general sense for what is actually a complex family of related ancient and modern living languages. Some Mayan words contain glottal stops, consonants that are spoken with a sharp burst of air from the constricted throat, similarly to how "k" sounds are made but more emphatically. When written, glottalized consonants are indicated with apostrophes (such as in "*k'in*"). Mayanists generally use the word "Maya" instead of "Mayan," except when referring to the languages of Maya peoples.

The intent of this small publication is to illustrate basic Maya calendar concepts as an introduction for further inquiry but there is much of this extensive subject that cannot be covered. What's included has been summarized from widely available sources from a century of scholarship and cannot necessarily represent every new groundbreaking idea. In the ever-evolving field of Maya studies, scholars often disagree and new ideas take time to settle out.

Muwan

Maya winal month name and glyph

2013 JANUARY

13.0.0.0.16

Long Counts for each day of 2013 are given in numeric notation (such as 13.0.0.0.16).

SUNDAY 6

7 Kib 19 K'ank'in

MONDAY 7

8 Kaban Seating Muwan

TUESDAY 8

The seating (first day) of each Maya month is noted with its glyph presented in dark reverse.

9 Ets'nab 1 Muwan

WEDNESDAY 9

This 365-k'in calendar

presents the year simultaneously with our standard 12-month Gregorian system and the Maya system of eighteen 20-day months. For practicality, Maya days are presented in 7-day Gregorian weeks.

10

Calendar Round dates are given for each day, both in text form and as Maya glyphs with bar-dot numerals. The seating day for each Maya month period is accentuated with the glyph for that month in solid black reverse.

The Long Count for the beginning of each week is presented glyphically in outside page margins.

Maya months are noted at the top of each page and distinguished by alternating colors of red and green.

Note – *Long Counts are given on assumption of moving forward into the 14th bak'tun of a 20-bak'tun (1 piktun) cycle rather than a reset to another 13-bak'tun cycle. With a 13-bak'tun cycle, all bak'tun coefficients would be 0 rather than 13 but all lower period coefficients would remain the same.*

K'ank'in

DECEMBER 2012

SUNDAY 16

12.19.19.17.15

12 Men 18 Mak

MONDAY 17

12.19.19.17.16

13 Kib 19 Mak

TUESDAY 18

12.19.19.17.17

1 Kaban Seating K'ank'in

WEDNESDAY 19

12.19.19.17.18

2 Ets'nab 1 K'ank'in

THURSDAY 20

12.19.19.17.19

3 Kawak 2 K'ank'in

FRIDAY 21

13.0.0.0.0

Completion of 13th bak'tun on Winter Solstice

13 bak'tuns 0 katuns 0 tuns 0 winals 0 k'ins 4 Ajaw 3 K'ank'in

SATURDAY 22

13.0.0.0.1

5 Imix 4 K'ank'in

DECEMBER

DECEMBER 2012

K'ank'in

23 SUNDAY

6 Ik' 5 K'ank'in

13.0.0.0.2

24 MONDAY

7 Ak'bal 6 K'ank'in   *Christmas Eve*   13.0.0.0.3

25 TUESDAY

8 K'an 7 K'ank'in   *Christmas Day*   13.0.0.0.4

26 WEDNESDAY

Copán Stela A
AD 731
Waxaklahun Ubah K'awil

9 Chikchan 8 K'ank'in   13.0.0.0.5

27 THURSDAY

10 Kimi 9 K'ank'in   13.0.0.0.6

28 FRIDAY

11 Manik 10 K'ank'in   13.0.0.0.7

29 SATURDAY

12 Lamat 11 K'ank'in   13.0.0.0.8

JANUARY 2013

K'ank'in

30 SUNDAY

13 Muluk 12 K'ank'in   13.0.0.0.9

31 MONDAY

1 Ok 13 K'ank'in   13.0.0.0.10

1 TUESDAY

2 Chuwen 14 K'ank'in   *New Year's Day*   13.0.0.0.11

2 WEDNESDAY

3 Eb 15 K'ank'in   13.0.0.0.12

3 THURSDAY

4 Ben 16 K'ank'in   13.0.0.0.13

4 FRIDAY

5 Ix 17 K'ank'in   ◐   13.0.0.0.14

5 SATURDAY

6 Men 18 K'ank'in   13.0.0.0.15

Muwan

2013 **JANUARY**

SUNDAY **6**

13.0.0.0.16 — 7 Kib 19 K'ank'in

MONDAY **7**

13.0.0.0.17 — 8 Kaban Seating Muwan

TUESDAY **8**

13.0.0.0.18 — 9 Ets'nab 1 Muwan

WEDNESDAY **9**

13.0.0.0.19 — 10 Kawak 2 Muwan

THURSDAY **10**

13.0.0.1.0 — 11 Ajaw 3 Muwan

FRIDAY **11**

13.0.0.1.1 — 12 Imix 4 Muwan

SATURDAY **12**

13.0.0.1.2 — 13 Ik' 5 Muwan

JANUARY 2013

Muwan

13 SUNDAY

1 Ak'bal 6 Muwan   13.0.0.1.3

14 MONDAY

2 K'an 7 Muwan   13.0.0.1.4

15 TUESDAY

3 Chikchan 8 Muwan   13.0.0.1.5

16 WEDNESDAY

4 Kimi 9 Muwan   13.0.0.1.6

17 THURSDAY

5 Manik 10 Muwan   13.0.0.1.7

18 FRIDAY

6 Lamat 11 Muwan   ◐   13.0.0.1.8

19 SATURDAY

7 Muluk 12 Muwan   13.0.0.1.9

JANUARY

Muwan

2013 **JANUARY**

SUNDAY **20**

13.0.0.1.10   8 Ok 13 Muwan

MONDAY **21**

13.0.0.1.11   *Martin Luther King, Jr. Day*   9 Chuwen 14 Muwan

TUESDAY **22**

13.0.0.1.12   10 Eb 15 Muwan

WEDNESDAY **23**

13.0.0.1.13   11 Ben 16 Muwan

THURSDAY **24**

13.0.0.1.14   12 Ix 17 Muwan

FRIDAY **25**

13.0.0.1.15   13 Men 18 Muwan

SATURDAY **26**

JANUARY

13.0.0.1.16   ○   1 Kib 19 Muwan

JAN / FEB 2013  Pax

27 SUNDAY

2 Kaban Seating Pax   13.0.0.1.17

28 MONDAY

3 Ets'nab 1 Pax   13.0.0.1.18

29 TUESDAY

4 Kawak 2 Pax   13.0.0.1.19

30 WEDNESDAY

Copán Stela P
AD 623
K'ak' Chan Yopaat

5 Ajaw 3 Pax   13.0.0.2.0

31 THURSDAY

6 Imix 4 Pax   13.0.0.2.1

1 FRIDAY

7 Ik' 5 Pax   13.0.0.2.2

2 SATURDAY

8 Ak'bal 6 Pax   13.0.0.2.3

February

FEBRUARY 2013

Pax

3 SUNDAY

9 K'an 7 Pax 13.0.0.2.4

4 MONDAY

10 Chikchan 8 Pax 13.0.0.2.5

5 TUESDAY

11 Kimi 9 Pax 13.0.0.2.6

6 WEDNESDAY

12 Manik 10 Pax 13.0.0.2.7

7 THURSDAY

13 Lamat 11 Pax 13.0.0.2.8

8 FRIDAY

1 Muluk 12 Pax 13.0.0.2.9

9 SATURDAY

2 Ok 13 Pax 13.0.0.2.10

Pax

2013 **FEBRUARY**

SUNDAY **10**

13.0.0.2.11

3 Chuwen 14 Pax

MONDAY **11**

13.0.0.2.12

4 Eb 15 Pax

TUESDAY **12**

13.0.0.2.13

5 Ben 16 Pax

WEDNESDAY **13**

13.0.0.2.14

6 Ix 17 Pax

THURSDAY **14**

13.0.0.2.15 *Valentine's Day*

7 Men 18 Pax

FRIDAY **15**

13.0.0.2.16

8 Kib 19 Pax

SATURDAY **16**

13.0.0.2.17

9 Kaban Seating Kayab

FEBRUARY 2013  K'ayab

17 SUNDAY

10 Ets'nab 1 Kayab   ◐   13.0.0.2.18

18 MONDAY

11 Kawak 2 Kayab   *Presidents' Day*   13.0.0.2.19

19 TUESDAY

12 Ajaw 3 Kayab   13.0.03.0

20 WEDNESDAY

13 Imix 4 Kayab   13.0.03.1

21 THURSDAY

1 Ik' 5 Kayab   13.0.03.2

22 FRIDAY

2 Ak'bal 6 Kayab   13.0.03.3

23 SATURDAY

3 K'an 7 Kayab   13.0.03.4

FEBRUARY

K'ayab

2013 **FEB / MAR**

SUNDAY 24

13.0.03.5   4 Chikchan 8 K'ayab

MONDAY 25

13.0.03.6   5 Kimi 9 K'ayab

TUESDAY 26

13.0.03.7   6 Manik 10 K'ayab

WEDNESDAY 27

13.0.03.8   7 Lamat 11 K'ayab

THURSDAY 28

13.0.03.9   8 Muluk 12 K'ayab

FRIDAY 1

13.0.03.10   9 Ok 13 K'ayab

SATURDAY 2

13.0.03.11   10 Chuwen 14 K'ayab

FEBRUARY / MARCH

MARCH 2013   K'ayab

3 SUNDAY

11 Eb 15 Kayab   13.0.03.12

4 MONDAY

12 Ben 16 Kayab   13.0.03.13

5 TUESDAY

13 Ix 17 Kayab   13.0.03.14

6 WEDNESDAY

Copán Stela D
AD 736
Waxaklahun Ubah K'awil

1 Men 18 Kayab   13.0.03.15

7 THURSDAY

 2 Kib 19 Kayab   13.0.03.16

8 FRIDAY

 3 Kaban Seating Kumku   13.0.03.17

9 SATURDAY

4 Ets'nab 1 Kumku   13.0.03.18

MARCH 2013

Kumk'u

10 SUNDAY

5 Kawak 2 Kumku   *Daylight Saving Time begins*   13.0.03.19

11 MONDAY

6 Ajaw 3 Kumku   13.0.04.0

12 TUESDAY

7 Imix 4 Kumku   13.0.04.1

13 WEDNESDAY

8 Ik' 5 Kumku   13.0.04.2

14 THURSDAY

9 Ak'bal 6 Kumku   13.0.04.3

15 FRIDAY

10 K'an 7 Kumku   13.0.04.4

16 SATURDAY

11 Chikchan 8 Kumku   13.0.04.5

Kumk'u

2013 **MARCH**

SUNDAY **17**

13.0.0.4.6

12 Kimi 9 Kumku

MONDAY **18**

13.0.04.7

13 Manik 10 Kumku

TUESDAY **19**

13.0.04.8 ◐

1 Lamat 11 Kumku

WEDNESDAY **20**

13.0.04.9 *Vernal Equinox*

2 Muluk 12 Kumku

THURSDAY **21**

13.0.04.10

3 Ok 13 Kumku

FRIDAY **22**

13.0.04.11

4 Chuwen 14 Kumku

SATURDAY **23**

13.0.04.12

5 Eb 15 Kumku

MARCH

MARCH 2013   Kumk'u

24 SUNDAY

6 Ben 16 Kumku   13.0.0.4.13

25 MONDAY

7 Ix 17 Kumku   13.0.0.4.14

26 TUESDAY

8 Men 18 Kumku   13.0.0.4.15

27 WEDNESDAY

Copán Stela B
AD 731
Waxaklahun Ubah K'awil

9 Kib 19 Kumku   13.0.0.4.16

28 THURSDAY

10 Kaban Seating Wayeb   *The special 5-day "unlucky" period of Wayeb begins*   13.0.0.4.17

29 FRIDAY

11 Ets'nab 1 Wayeb   13.0.0.4.18

30 SATURDAY

12 Kawak 2 Wayeb   13.0.0.4.19

APRIL 2013

Wayeb

31 SUNDAY

13 Ajaw 3 Wayeb   Easter Sunday   13.0.0.5.0

1 MONDAY

1 Imix 4 Wayeb   April Fool's Day   13.0.0.5.1

2 TUESDAY

2 Ik' Seating Pop   "New Year's" day for the
                              365-day Haab calendar cycle   13.0.0.5.2

3 WEDNESDAY

3 Ak'bal 1 Pop   13.0.0.5.3

4 THURSDAY

4 K'an 2 Pop   13.0.0.5.4

5 FRIDAY

5 Chikchan 3 Pop   13.0.0.5.5

6 SATURDAY

6 Kimi 4 Pop   13.0.0.5.6

MARCH / APRIL

Pop

2013 **APRIL**

SUNDAY **7**

13.0.0.5.7

7 Manik 5 Pop

MONDAY **8**

13.0.0.5.8

8 Lamat 6 Pop

TUESDAY **9**

13.0.0.5.9

9 Muluk 7 Pop

WEDNESDAY **10**

13.0.0.5.10

10 Ok 8 Pop

THURSDAY **11**

13.0.0.5.11

11 Chuwen 9 Pop

FRIDAY **12**

13.0.0.5.12

12 Eb 10 Pop

SATURDAY **13**

13.0.0.5.13

13 Ben 11 Pop

APRIL

APRIL 2013

Pop

14 SUNDAY

1 Ix 12 Pop   13.0.0.5.14

15 MONDAY

2 Men 13 Pop   13.0.0.5.15

16 TUESDAY

3 Kib 14 Pop   13.0.0.5.16

17 WEDNESDAY

4 Kaban 15 Pop   13.0.0.5.17

18 THURSDAY

5 Ets'nab 16 Pop   13.0.0.5.18

19 FRIDAY

6 Kawak 17 Pop   13.0.0.5.19

20 SATURDAY

7 Ajaw 18 Pop   13.0.0.6.0

APRIL

Wo

2013 **APRIL**

SUNDAY **21**

13.0.0.6.1
8 Imix 19 Pop

MONDAY **22**

13.0.0.6.2
9 Ik' Seating Wo

TUESDAY **23**

13.0.0.6.3
10 Ak'bal 1 Wo

WEDNESDAY **24**

13.0.0.6.4
11 K'an 2 Wo

THURSDAY **25**

13.0.0.6.5
12 Chikchan 3 Wo

FRIDAY **26**

13.0.0.6.6
13 Kimi 4 Wo

SATURDAY **27**

13.0.0.6.7
1 Manik 5 Wo

APRIL

APRIL / MAY 2013  Wo

28 SUNDAY

2 Lamat 6 Wo   13.0.0.6.8

29 MONDAY

3 Muluk 7 Wo   13.0.0.6.9

30 TUESDAY

4 Ok 8 Wo   13.0.0.6.10

1 WEDNESDAY

Copán Stela I
AD 676
"Smoke Imix"

5 Chuwen 9 Wo   *May Day*   13.0.0.6.11

2 THURSDAY

6 Eb 10 Wo   13.0.0.6.12

3 FRIDAY

7 Ben 11 Wo   13.0.0.6.13

4 SATURDAY

8 Ix 12 Wo   13.0.0.6.14

MAY 2013

Wo

5 SUNDAY

9 Men 13 Wo   *Cinco de Mayo*   13.0.0.6.15

6 MONDAY

10 Kib 14 Wo   13.0.0.6.16

7 TUESDAY

11 Kaban 15 Wo   13.0.0.6.17

8 WEDNESDAY

12 Ets'nab 16 Wo   13.0.0.6.18

9 THURSDAY

13 Kawak 17 Wo   13.0.0.6.19

10 FRIDAY

1 Ajaw 18 Wo   13.0.0.7.0

11 SATURDAY

2 Imix 19 Wo   13.0.0.7.1

Sip

2013 **MAY**

SUNDAY **12**

13.0.0.7.2   *Mother's Day*   3 Ik' Seating Sip

MONDAY **13**

13.0.0.7.3   4 Ak'bal 1 Sip

TUESDAY **14**

13.0.0.7.4   5 K'an 2 Sip

WEDNESDAY **15**

13.0.0.7.5   6 Chikchan 3 Sip

THURSDAY **16**

13.0.0.7.6   7 Kimi 4 Sip

FRIDAY **17**

13.0.0.7.7   8 Manik 5 Sip

SATURDAY **18**

13.0.0.7.8   9 Lamat 6 Sip

MAY 2013

 Sip

19 SUNDAY

10 Muluk 7 Sip   13.0.0.7.9

20 MONDAY

11 Ok 8 Sip   13.0.0.7.10

21 TUESDAY

12 Chuwen 9 Sip   13.0.0.7.11

22 WEDNESDAY

13 Eb 10 Sip   *Earth Day*   13.0.0.7.12

23 THURSDAY

1 Ben 11 Sip   13.0.0.7.13

24 FRIDAY

2 Ix 12 Sip   13.0.0.7.14

25 SATURDAY

3 Men 13 Sip   13.0.0.7.15

Sip

2013 **MAY**

SUNDAY **26**

13.0.0.7.16 — 4 Kib 14 Sip

MONDAY **27**

13.0.0.7.17 — *Memorial Day* — 5 Kaban 15 Sip

TUESDAY **28**

13.0.0.7.18 — 6 Ets'nab 16 Sip

WEDNESDAY **29**

13.0.0.7.19 — 7 Kawak 17 Sip

THURSDAY **30**

13.0.0.8.0 — 8 Ajaw 18 Sip

FRIDAY **31**

13.0.0.8.1 — 9 Imix 19 Sip

SATURDAY **1**

13.0.0.8.2 — 10 Ik' Seating Sots

MAY / JUNE

JUNE 2013

Sots

2 SUNDAY

11 Ak'bal 1 Sots'   13.0.0.8.3

3 MONDAY

12 K'an 2 Sots'   13.0.0.8.4

4 TUESDAY

13 Chikchan 3 Sots'   13.0.0.8.5

5 WEDNESDAY

Copán Stela H
AD 730
Waxaklahun Ubah K'awil

1 Kimi 4 Sots'   13.0.0.8.6

6 THURSDAY

2 Manik 5 Sots'   13.0.0.8.7

7 FRIDAY

3 Lamat 6 Sots'   13.0.0.8.8

8 SATURDAY

4 Muluk 7 Sots'   13.0.0.8.9

JUNE 2013  Sots

9 SUNDAY

5 Ok 8 Sots'   13.0.0.8.10

10 MONDAY

6 Chuwen 9 Sots'   13.0.0.8.11

11 TUESDAY

7 Eb 10 Sots'   13.0.0.8.12

12 WEDNESDAY

8 Ben 11 Sots'   13.0.0.8.13

13 THURSDAY

9 Ix 12 Sots'   13.0.0.8.14

14 FRIDAY

10 Men 13 Sots'   13.0.0.8.15

15 SATURDAY

11 Kib 14 Sots'   13.0.0.8.16

Sots

2013 **JUNE**

SUNDAY **16**

13.0.0.8.17 *Father's Day* 12 Kaban 15 Sots'

MONDAY **17**

13.0.0.8.18 13 Ets'nab 16 Sots'

TUESDAY **18**

13.0.0.8.19 1 Kawak 17 Sots'

WEDNESDAY **19**

13.0.0.9.0 2 Ajaw 18 Sots'

THURSDAY **20**

13.0.0.9.1 3 Imix 19 Sots'

FRIDAY **21**

13.0.0.9.2 *Summer Solstice* 4 Ik' Seating Sek

SATURDAY **22**

13.0.0.9.3 5 Ak'bal 1 Sek

JUNE

JUNE 2013

Sek

23 SUNDAY

6 K'an 2 Sek   13.0.0.9.4

24 MONDAY

7 Chikchan 3 Sek   13.0.0.9.5

25 TUESDAY

8 Kimi 4 Sek   13.0.0.9.6

26 WEDNESDAY

Copán Stela F
AD 721
Waxaklahun Ubah K'awil

9 Manik 5 Sek   13.0.0.9.7

27 THURSDAY

10 Lamat 6 Sek   13.0.0.9.8

28 FRIDAY

11 Muluk 7 Sek   13.0.0.9.9

29 SATURDAY

12 Ok 8 Sek   13.0.0.9.10

JUNE

JULY 2013

Sek

30 SUNDAY

13 Chuwen 9 Sek — 13.0.0.9.11

1 MONDAY

1 Eb 10 Sek — 13.0.0.9.12

2 TUESDAY

2 Ben 11 Sek — 13.0.0.9.13

3 WEDNESDAY

3 Ix 12 Sek — 13.0.0.9.14

4 THURSDAY

4 Men 13 Sek — *Independence Day* — 13.0.0.9.15

5 FRIDAY

5 Kib 14 Sek — 13.0.0.9.16

6 SATURDAY

6 Kaban 15 Sek — 13.0.0.9.17

JUNE / JULY

Sek

2013 **JULY**

SUNDAY 7

13.0.0.9.18

7 Ets'nab 16 Sek

MONDAY 8

13.0.0.9.19

8 Kawak 17 Sek

TUESDAY 9

13.0.0.10.0

9 Ajaw 18 Sek

WEDNESDAY 10

13.0.0.10.1

10 Imix 19 Sek

THURSDAY 11

13.0.0.10.2

11 Ik' Seating Xul

FRIDAY 12

13.0.0.10.3

12 Ak'bal 1 Xul

SATURDAY 13

13.0.0.10.4

13 K'an 2 Xul

JULY 2013   Xul

14 SUNDAY

1 Chikchan 3 Xul   13.0.0.10.5

15 MONDAY

2 Kimi 4 Xul   ◐   13.0.0.10.6

16 TUESDAY

3 Manik 5 Xul   13.0.0.10.7

17 WEDNESDAY

4 Lamat 6 Xul   13.0.0.10.8

18 THURSDAY

5 Muluk 7 Xul   13.0.0.10.9

19 FRIDAY

6 Ok 8 Xul   13.0.0.10.10

20 SATURDAY

7 Chuwen 9 Xul   13.0.0.10.11

JULY

Xul

2013 **JULY**

SUNDAY **21**

13.0.0.10.12   8 Eb 10 Xul

MONDAY **22**

13.0.0.10.13   9 Ben 11 Xul

TUESDAY **23**

13.0.0.10.14   10 Ix 12 Xul

WEDNESDAY **24**

13.0.0.10.15   11 Men 13 Xul

THURSDAY **25**

13.0.0.10.16   12 Kib 14 Xul

FRIDAY **26**

13.0.0.10.17   13 Kaban 15 Xul

SATURDAY **27**

13.0.0.10.18   1 Ets'nab 16 Xul

JULY / AUG 2013  Xul

28 SUNDAY

2 Kawak 17 Xul — 13.0.0.10.19

29 MONDAY

3 Ajaw 18 Xul — 13.0.0.11.0

30 TUESDAY

4 Imix 19 Xul — 13.0.0.11.1

31 WEDNESDAY

Copán Stela C
AD 711
Waxaklahun Ubah K'awil

5 Ik' Seating Yaxk'in — 13.0.0.11.2

1 THURSDAY

6 Ak'bal 1 Yaxk'in — 13.0.0.11.3

2 FRIDAY

7 K'an 2 Yaxk'in — 13.0.0.11.4

3 SATURDAY

8 Chikchan 3 Yaxk'in — 13.0.0.11.5

August

AUGUST 2013

Yaxk'in

4 SUNDAY

9 Kimi 4 Yaxk'in   13.0.0.11.6

5 MONDAY

10 Manik 5 Yaxk'in   13.0.0.11.7

6 TUESDAY

11 Lamat 6 Yaxk'in   13.0.0.11.8

7 WEDNESDAY

12 Muluk 7 Yaxk'in   13.0.0.11.9

8 THURSDAY

13 Ok 8 Yaxk'in   13.0.0.11.10

9 FRIDAY

1 Chuwen 9 Yaxk'in   13.0.0.11.11

10 SATURDAY

2 Eb 10 Yaxk'in   13.0.0.11.12

Yaxk'in

2013 **AUGUST**

SUNDAY **11**

13.0.0.11.13 — 3 Ben 11 Yaxk'in

MONDAY **12**

13.0.0.11.14 — 4 Ix 12 Yaxk'in

TUESDAY **13**

13.0.0.11.15 — 5 Men 13 Yaxk'in

WEDNESDAY **14**

13.0.0.11.16  6 Kib 14 Yaxk'in

THURSDAY **15**

13.0.0.11.17 — 7 Kaban 15 Yaxk'in

FRIDAY **16**

13.0.0.11.18 — 8 Ets'nab 16 Yaxk'in

SATURDAY **17**

13.0.0.11.19 — 9 Kawak 17 Yaxk'in

AUGUST

AUGUST 2013

Mol

18 SUNDAY

10 Ajaw 18 Yaxk'in   13.0.0.12.0

19 MONDAY

11 Imix 19 Yaxk'in   13.0.0.12.1

20 TUESDAY

12 Ik' Seating Mol   13.0.0.12.2

21 WEDNESDAY

13 Ak'bal 1 Mol   13.0.0.12.3

22 THURSDAY

1 K'an 2 Mol   13.0.0.12.4

23 FRIDAY

12 Chikchan 3 Mol   13.0.0.12.5

24 SATURDAY

3 Kimi 4 Mol   13.0.0.12.6

Mol

2013 **AUGUST**

SUNDAY **25**

13.0.0.12.7 — 4 Manik 5 Mol

MONDAY **26**

13.0.0.12.8 — 5 Lamat 6 Mol

TUESDAY **27**

13.0.0.12.9 — 6 Muluk 7 Mol

WEDNESDAY **28**

13.0.0.12.10 — 7 Ok 8 Mol

THURSDAY **29**

13.0.0.12.11 — 8 Chuwen 9 Mol

FRIDAY **30**

13.0.0.12.12 — 9 Eb 10 Mol

SATURDAY **31**

13.0.0.12.13 — 10 Ben 11 Mol

SEPTEMBER 2013

Mol

1 SUNDAY

11 Ix 12 Mol

13.0.0.12.14

2 MONDAY

12 Men 13 Mol *Labor Day*

13.0.0.12.15

3 TUESDAY

13 Kib 14 Mol

13.0.0.12.16

4 WEDNESDAY

Quirigua Stela C
AD 775
K'ak' Tiliw

1 Kaban 15 Mol

13.0.0.12.17

5 THURSDAY

2 Ets'nab 16 Mol

13.0.0.12.18

6 FRIDAY

3 Kawak 17 Mol

13.0.0.12.19

7 SATURDAY

4 Ajaw 18 Mol

13.0.0.13.0

September

SEPTEMBER 2013

Ch'en

8 SUNDAY

5 Imix 19 Mol   13.0.0.13.1

9 MONDAY

6 Ik' Seating Ch'en   13.0.0.13.2

10 TUESDAY

7 Ak'bal 1 Ch'en   13.0.0.13.3

11 WEDNESDAY

8 K'an 2 Ch'en   13.0.0.13.4

12 THURSDAY

9 Chikchan 3 Ch'en   ◐   13.0.0.13.5

13 FRIDAY

10 Kimi 4 Ch'en   13.0.0.13.6

14 SATURDAY

11 Manik 5 Ch'en   13.0.0.13.7

Ch'en

2013 SEPTEMBER

SUNDAY **15**

13.0.0.13.8

12 Lamat 6 Ch'en

MONDAY **16**

13.0.0.13.9

13 Muluk 7 Ch'en

TUESDAY **17**

13.0.0.13.10

1 Ok 8 Ch'en

WEDNESDAY **18**

13.0.0.13.11

2 Chuwen 9 Ch'en

THURSDAY **19**

13.0.0.13.12

3 Eb 10 Ch'en

FRIDAY **20**

13.0.0.13.13

4 Ben 11 Ch'en

SATURDAY **21**

13.0.0.13.14

5 Ix 12 Ch'en

SEPTEMBER

SEPTEMBER 2013

Ch'en

22 SUNDAY

6 Men 13 Ch'en   *Autumnal Equinox*   13.0.0.13.15

23 MONDAY

7 Kib 14 Ch'en   13.0.0.13.16

24 TUESDAY

8 Kaban 15 Ch'en   13.0.0.13.17

25 WEDNESDAY

Quirigua Stela E
AD 725
K'ak' Tiliw

9 Ets'nab 16 Ch'en   13.0.0.13.18

26 THURSDAY

◐

10 Kawak 17 Ch'en   13.0.0.13.19

27 FRIDAY

11 Ajaw 18 Ch'en   13.0.0.14.0

28 SATURDAY

12 Imix 19 Ch'en   13.0.0.14.1

SEP / OCT 2013

Yax

29 SUNDAY

13 Ik' Seating Yax   13.0.0.14.2

30 MONDAY

1 Ak'bal 1 Yax   13.0.0.14.3

1 TUESDAY

2 K'an 2 Yax   13.0.0.14.4

2 WEDNESDAY

3 Chikchan 3 Yax   13.0.0.14.5

3 THURSDAY

4 Kimi 4 Yax   13.0.0.14.6

4 FRIDAY

5 Manik 5 Yax   13.0.0.14.7

5 SATURDAY

6 Lamat 6 Yax   13.0.0.14.8

SEPTEMBER / OCTOBER

Yax

	SUNDAY	6

13.0.0.14.9

 7 Muluk 7 Yax

	MONDAY	7

13.0.0.14.10

 8 Ok 8 Yax

	TUESDAY	8

13.0.0.14.11

 9 Chuwen 9 Yax

	WEDNESDAY	9

13.0.0.14.12

 10 Eb 10 Yax

	THURSDAY	10

13.0.0.14.13

 11 Ben 11 Yax

	FRIDAY	11

13.0.0.14.14

 12 Ix 12 Yax

	SATURDAY	12

13.0.0.14.15

 13 Men 13 Yax

OCTOBER

OCTOBER 2013

Yax

13 SUNDAY

1 Kib 14 Yax   13.0.0.14.16

14 MONDAY

2 Kaban 15 Yax   *Columbus Day*   13.0.0.14.17

15 TUESDAY

3 Ets'nab 16 Yax   13.0.0.14.18

16 WEDNESDAY

4 Kawak 17 Yax   13.0.0.14.19

17 THURSDAY

5 Ajaw 18 Yax   13.0.0.15.0

18 FRIDAY

6 Imix 19 Yax   13.0.0.15.1

19 SATURDAY

7 Ik' Seating Sak   13.0.0.15.2

OCTOBER

Sak

2013 **OCTOBER**

SUNDAY **20**

13.0.0.15.3   8 Ak'bal 1 Sak

MONDAY **21**

13.0.0.15.4   9 K'an 2 Sak

TUESDAY **22**

13.0.0.15.5   10 Chikchan 3 Sak

WEDNESDAY **23**

13.0.0.15.6   11 Kimi 4 Sak

THURSDAY **24**

13.0.0.15.7   12 Manik 5 Sak

FRIDAY **25**

13.0.0.15.8   13 Lamat 6 Sak

SATURDAY **26**

13.0.0.15.9   1 Muluk 7 Sak

OCTOBER

OCT / NOV 2013  Sak

27 SUNDAY

2 Ok 8 Sak · 13.0.0.15.10

28 MONDAY

3 Chuwen 9 Sak · 13.0.0.15.11

29 TUESDAY

4 Eb 10 Sak · 13.0.0.15.12

30 WEDNESDAY

Quirigua Stela D
AD 766
K'ak' Tiliw

5 Ben 11 Sak · 13.0.0.15.13

31 THURSDAY

6 Ix 12 Sak · · · · · · · · · · · · · · · *Halloween* · 13.0.0.15.14

1 FRIDAY

7 Men 13 Sak · 13.0.0.15.15

2 SATURDAY

8 Kib 14 Sak · 13.0.0.15.16

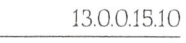

November

NOVEMBER 2013

 Sak

3 SUNDAY

9 Kaban 15 Sak

 Daylight Saving Time Ends   13.0.0.15.17

4 MONDAY

10 Ets'nab 16 Sak   13.0.0.15.18

5 TUESDAY

11 Kawak 17 Sak   13.0.0.15.19

6 WEDNESDAY

12 Ajaw 18 Sak   13.0.0.16.0

7 THURSDAY

13 Imix 19 Sak   13.0.0.16.1

8 FRIDAY

1 Ik' Seating Keh   13.0.0.16.2

9 SATURDAY

2 Ak'bal 1 Keh   13.0.0.16.3

NOVEMBER

Keh

2013 **NOVEMBER**

SUNDAY **10**

13.0.0.16.4   3 K'an 2 Keh

MONDAY **11**

13.0.0.16.5   *Veteran's Day*   4 Chikchan 3 Keh

TUESDAY **12**

13.0.0.16.6   5 Kimi 4 Keh

WEDNESDAY **13**

13.0.0.16.7   6 Manik 5 Keh

THURSDAY **14**

13.0.0.16.8   7 Lamat 6 Keh

FRIDAY **15**

13.0.0.16.9   8 Muluk 7 Keh

SATURDAY **16**

13.0.0.16.10   9 Ok 8 Keh

NOVEMBER 2013  Keh

17 SUNDAY

10 Chuwen 9 Kèh   13.0.0.16.11

18 MONDAY

11 Eb 10 Kèh   13.0.0.16.12

19 TUESDAY

12 Ben 11 Kèh   13.0.0.16.13

20 WEDNESDAY

13 Ix 12 Kèh   13.0.0.16.14

21 THURSDAY

1 Men 13 Kèh   13.0.0.16.15

22 FRIDAY

2 Kib 14 Kèh   13.0.0.16.16

23 SATURDAY

3 Kaban 15 Kèh   13.0.0.16.17

Keh

2013 **NOVEMBER**

SUNDAY **24**

13.0.0.16.18   4 Ets'nab 16 Keh

MONDAY **25**

13.0.0.16.19   5 Kawak 17 Keh

TUESDAY **26**

13.0.0.17.0   6 Ajaw 18 Keh

WEDNESDAY **27**

13.0.0.17.1   7 Imix 19 Keh

THURSDAY **28**

13.0.0.17.2   *Thanksgiving*   8 Ik' Seating Mak

FRIDAY **29**

13.0.0.17.3   9 Ak'bal 1 Mak

SATURDAY **30**

13.0.0.17.4   10 K'an 2 Mak

DECEMBER 2013

Mak

1 SUNDAY

11 Chikchan 3 Mak   13.0.0.17.5

2 MONDAY

12 Kimi 4 Mak   13.0.0.17.6

3 TUESDAY

13 Manik 5 Mak   13.0.0.17.7

4 WEDNESDAY

Quirigua Zoomorph P
AD 795
"Sky Xul"

1 Lamat 6 Mak   13.0.0.17.8

5 THURSDAY

2 Muluk 7 Mak   13.0.0.17.9

6 FRIDAY

3 Ok 8 Mak   13.0.0.17.10

7 SATURDAY

4 Chuwen 9 Mak   13.0.0.17.11

December

DECEMBER 2013   Mak

8 SUNDAY

5 Eb 10 Mak   13.0.0.17.12

9 MONDAY

6 Ben 11 Mak   13.0.0.17.13

10 TUESDAY

7 Ix 12 Mak   13.0.0.17.14

11 WEDNESDAY

8 Men 13 Mak   13.0.0.17.15

12 THURSDAY

9 Kib 14 Mak   13.0.0.17.16

13 FRIDAY

10 Kaban 15 Mak   13.0.0.17.17

14 SATURDAY

11 Ets'nab 16 Mak   13.0.0.17.18

Mak

2013 DECEMBER

SUNDAY **15**

13.0.0.17.19

12 Kawak 17 Mak

MONDAY **16**

13.0.1.0.0

13 Ajaw 18 Mak

TUESDAY **17**

13.0.1.0.1

1 Imix 19 Mak

WEDNESDAY **18**

13.0.1.0.2

2 Ik' Seating K'ank'in

THURSDAY **19**

13.0.1.0.3

3 Ak'bal 1 K'ank'in

FRIDAY **20**

13.0.1.0.4

4 K'an 2 K'ank'in

SATURDAY **21**

13.0.1.0.5   *Winter Solstice*

5 Chikchan 3 K'ank'in

DECEMBER 2013

K'ank'in

22 SUNDAY

6 Kimi 4 K'ank'in   13.0.1.0.6

23 MONDAY

7 Manik 5 K'ank'in   13.0.1.0.7

24 TUESDAY

8 Lamat 6 K'ank'in   *Christmas Eve*   13.0.1.0.8

25 WEDNESDAY

9 Muluk 7 K'ank'in   *Christmas Day*   13.0.1.0.9

26 THURSDAY

10 Ok 8 K'ank'in   13.0.1.0.10

27 FRIDAY

11 Chuwen 9 K'ank'in   13.0.1.0.11

28 SATURDAY

12 Eb 10 K'ank'in   13.0.1.0.12

DECEMBER

K'ank'in

2013 **DECEMBER**

SUNDAY **29**

13.0.1.0.13   13 Ben 11 K'ank'in

MONDAY **30**

13.0.1.0.14   1 Ix 12 K'ank'in

TUESDAY **31**

13.0.1.0.15   *New Year's Eve*   2 Men 13 K'ank'in

Maya calendar 2013

Maya month glyphs and their corresponding Gregorian dates are printed in alternating tones of red and green.

		S	M	T	W	T	F	S	
MUWAN				1	2	3	4	5	JAN
		6	7	8	9	10	11	12	
		13	14	15	16	17	18	19	
		20	21	22	23	24	25	26	
PAX		27	28	29	30	31	1	2	FEB
		3	4	5	6	7	8	9	
		10	11	12	13	14	15	16	
KAYAB		17	18	19	20	21	22	23	
		24	25	26	27	28	1	2	MAR
		3	4	5	6	7	8	9	
KUMKU		10	11	12	13	14	15	16	
		17	18	19	20	21	22	23	
WAYEB		24	25	26	27	28	29	30	
		31	1	2	3	4	5	6	APR
POP		7	8	9	10	11	12	13	
		14	15	16	17	18	19	20	
		21	22	23	24	25	26	27	
WO		28	29	30	1	2	3	4	MAY
		5	6	7	8	9	10	11	
SIP		12	13	14	15	16	17	18	
		19	20	21	22	23	24	25	
		26	27	28	29	30	31	1	JUN
SOTS'		2	3	4	5	6	7	8	
		9	10	11	12	13	14	15	
		16	17	18	19	20	21	22	
SEK		23	24	25	26	27	28	29	
		30							

2013 Maya calendar

	S	M	T	W	T	F	S	
JUL		1	2	3	4	5	6	
	7	8	9	10	11	12	13	XUL
	14	15	16	17	18	19	20	
	21	22	23	24	25	26	27	
	28	29	30	31	1	2	3	YAXKIN
AUG	4	5	6	7	8	9	10	
	11	12	13	14	15	16	17	
	18	19	20	21	22	23	24	MOL
	25	26	27	28	29	30	31	
SEP	1	2	3	4	5	6	7	
	8	9	10	11	12	13	14	CH'EN
	15	16	17	18	19	20	21	
	22	23	24	25	26	27	28	
	29	30	1	2	3	4	5	YAX
OCT	6	7	8	9	10	11	12	
	13	14	15	16	17	18	19	SAK
	20	21	22	23	24	25	26	
	27	28	29	30	31	1	2	
NOV	3	4	5	6	7	8	9	
	10	11	12	13	14	15	16	KEH
	17	18	19	20	21	22	23	
	24	25	26	27	28	29	30	
DEC	1	2	3	4	5	6	7	MAK
	8	9	10	11	12	13	14	
	15	16	17	18	19	20	21	
	22	23	24	25	26	27	28	KANKIN
	29	30	31					

©2012 Ancientime
Except as noted, all illustrations and photographs in this calendar
were created and are copyrighted by the author.

Full-figure glyph on page 1 and Quirigua Stela C Long Count glyphs on
page 22 drawn with reference to the ca. 1900 work of Annie G. Hunter
for Alfred P. Maudslay's *Biologia Centrali-Americana*.
Page 17 Calendar Round graphic incorporates a NASA photo of
the Crab Nebula region (NASA / ESA / Hubble / Davide De Martin)
Page 24 Cobá stela 1 drawing after Linda Schele and Ian Graham.
Page 27 Tortuguero monument 6 drawing after Sven Grönemeyer and
Mark Van Stone, and photos by Donald Hales and Elisabeth Wagner.

*The intent of this calendar is educational. Every effort has been made to ensure
accuracy but no responsibility is accepted for inaccuracies or ommisions.*